# writing guides

ACTIVITIES

C000015705

# Persuasive WRITING

### CHRIS LUTRARIO

PHOTOCOPIABLE PHOTO

**NON-FICTION FOR AGES 9–11**

# CONTENTS

## INTRODUCTION

The Scholastic *Writing Guides* series provides teachers with ideas and projects that promote a range of writing, bringing insights from educational research into the classroom. Each guide explores a different type of writing and provides example material, background information, photocopiable activities and teaching suggestions. Their aim is to enable teachers to guide the writing process, share planning ideas and develop themes as a context for writing activities.

The materials:
- motivate children with interesting activities
- break complex types of writing into manageable teaching units
- focus on and develop the typical features of particular types of writing
- provide original approaches to teaching.

Each book is divided into sections, beginning with examples of the type of writing being taught. These are followed by ideas for developing writing and projects that will extend over a series of sessions.

## SECTION ONE: USING GOOD EXAMPLES

Section One looks at good examples of the genre, with the emphasis on using texts to stimulate and develop writing. Two example texts are shared, and questions that focus the discussion on their significant features are suggested. This is followed by activities that explore what the texts can teach us about writing, enabling teachers to compare the two texts and to go on to model the type of writing presented in the guide.

## SECTION TWO: DEVELOPING WRITING

Section Two moves from reading to writing. This section provides activities that prompt and support children in planning and writing. A range of approaches includes planning templates and strategies to stimulate ideas. The activities refine children's ideas about the type of writing being developed and give them focused writing practice in the context of scaffolded tasks. Teacher's notes support each activity by explaining the objective and giving guidance on delivery.

## SECTION THREE: WRITING

Section Three moves on to writing projects. Building upon the earlier work in Section Two, these projects aim to develop the quality of writing and provide a selection of ideas for class or group work on a particular theme or idea. The teacher may choose to use some or all of the ideas presented in each project as a way of weaving the strategies developed in Section Two into a more complex and extended writing task.

## SECTION FOUR: REVIEW

Section Four supports the assessment process. Children are encouraged to reflect on the type of writing they are tackling and to evaluate how effectively their work has met the criteria for the genre identified in Section One.

# The smacking debate

Dear Editor

We have been following the correspondence in your newspaper about the proposal to introduce a law banning the smacking of children. Our view is that smacking can never be justified, and that there are strong arguments in favour of such a law.

Firstly, it is not true, as the pro-smackers like to claim, that 'smacking works'. It might frighten a child into 'being good' for a while, but the effect is not likely to last long. Smacking doesn't work because it cannot change behaviour, and that should be the aim. To change someone's behaviour we need to talk with them, to show them why their behaviour is wrong, and to help them change it.

Secondly, we need to consider what message smacking sends. A smack teaches children the lesson that violence is the answer to every problem. We should not, therefore, be surprised if they go on to use violence themselves in other situations. Furthermore, smacking tells children that it is all right for the strong (in this case, adults) to exercise power over the weak (in this case, children). These are not the lessons we want them to learn if we value respect and consideration for others and want to build caring communities.

A third argument for banning smacking is a practical rather than a moral one. Smacking can result in serious injury. Adults might intend to give a child a quick, sharp smack. However, a smack can turn into a blow that causes real harm. This is especially the case if the smack is administered when the adult has lost their temper and aimed at the head. The only way to avoid this risk is not to smack at all.

We believe that these arguments show clearly that smacking is not an effective punishment and indeed has the potential to do great harm. A law banning it should be passed as soon as possible.

Yours sincerely
*Tofayel Hussain and Lacey Harman (age 11)*

# GIVE YOUR CAR A BREAK!

A quarter of all journeys are less than 2 miles long. School-run journeys make up 20% of all car journeys in the morning rush hour.

## SO...???
## Take the train. Take the bus. Or take a walk!

### WHY...???
**BECAUSE** it's good for your health.
Medical research shows that physically inactive people run **TWICE** the risk of heart disease. Make sure your car doesn't kill you.

### WHY...???
**BECAUSE** it's good for other people's health.
Particles in vehicle emissions aggravate heart and lung problems, and can even lead to early death.
Make sure your car doesn't kill your neighbours.

### WHY...???
**BECAUSE** it cuts congestion.
Traffic jams might make you fret and fume. But did you know that they also cost British industry £20 billion (yes, that's right, £20,000,000,000!) every single year? Make sure your car doesn't cost you **YOUR JOB**.

### WHY...???
**BECAUSE** public transport takes up much less space than travel in private cars. A full bus can carry as many people as 50 cars. And that's **A LOT LESS** pollution.

*Persuasive writing takes many forms, for example advertisements and brochures; leaflets and posters related to campaigns; editorials and letters in newspapers and magazines. The purpose of all these is to persuade the reader to adopt a particular point of view and also sometimes to take action. It is therefore a kind of writing that prompts writers to focus on their audience and to consider the likely power and effect of their words.*

*Persuasive texts also vary in structure and style, depending on how the writer sets out to achieve his or her aim. They can be cool and reasoned, for example in an editorial in which a view is stated and then supported by means of logical argument and relevant evidence. They can be dramatic and emotive, for example in a campaign leaflet that uses exaggeration and plays on the reader's feelings. At the extreme, persuasive writing can become manipulative, even dishonest, for example when evidence is distorted or opinions are presented as facts.*

## Sharing the persuasive texts

### The smacking debate

This first text is a letter to the editor of a newspaper arguing in favour of a ban on smacking. It is clearly organised and the tone is calm and rational.

Before sharing the text, share the children's thoughts on the rights and wrongs of smacking. Display an OHT or enlarged copy of the text, and ask them to identify the type of writing and its context. Give them time to read the letter independently. Ask them to summarise the basic position of the authors, and the arguments used to support it. Discuss how this relates to the structure of the letter: an introductory paragraph stating the main point; three paragraphs, each focusing on a supporting argument, which is developed through explanation and logical reasoning; a concluding paragraph summarising the arguments. Note that only one point of view is considered and that no factual evidence is put forward to support it.

Re-read the letter, focusing on language and style. Draw attention to words that structure the argument (*firstly, secondly, furthermore* and so on); and to words and phrases that make logical connections (*but, because, therefore* and so on). Encourage the children also to comment on the letter's general tone, clarity and effectiveness.

### Give your car a break!

This leaflet is designed to persuade people to use their cars less. Like the first text, it puts forward only one view and is clearly organised. However, unlike the letter, it makes use of design features and persuasive devices.

Begin by asking the children to identify the type of text and its purpose, and contexts in which they have met similar texts. Ask what they notice about its structure (question-and-answer format, repeated patterns, introductory statements followed by supporting arguments and evidence) and appearance (use of different typefaces and sizes and illustrations). Discuss how this is designed to catch readers' attention and draw them in.

Focus in on the sentence *Make sure your car doesn't kill you.* Ask the children what effect this creates. Find and discuss other examples of emotive and dramatic uses of language (*early death, cost you YOUR JOB, yes, that's right,* the alliteration of *fret and fume,* the use of imperatives). Discuss how such devices are designed to manipulate the reader's thoughts and feelings.

Ask the children how the position is supported. Draw out the idea that this is largely through citing factual evidence. Identify examples of this and consider how convincing they are.

## How persuasive texts work

The grid provided on photocopiable page 8 is designed to help focus and structure the analysis of persuasive texts. Display OHTs or enlarged copies alongside the texts on photocopiable pages 4 and 5. Prompt the children to focus on the points raised, and use shared-writing techniques to complete the grid for each text.

## The smacking debate – continued

Photocopiable page 9 provides the beginning of a reply to the letter on photocopiable page 4, and takes an opposing point of view. Identify its purpose, organisation and content. Examine how it is written and how it differs from the first letter. Draw attention to the use of such devices as persuasive wordings (*tried-and-tested practice*); making assumptions (*No, of course you wouldn't, every sensible parent*); exaggeration (*total nonsense*); rhetorical questions (*Would you talk with them...? And why?*); the dramatic opening; the choice of example (touching a hot iron).

Complete the letter as a shared-writing activity. This involves expressing arguments against the next two points in the original letter. Encourage them to try to sustain the tone and style of the reply, and to make use of similar persuasive devices.

# Taking ideas further

## What kind of writing?

Persuasive texts take many different forms and can be written in many different styles and tones, depending on the specific aims that their authors have in mind and the devices they think will be most appropriate and effective. The activity on photocopiable page 10 is designed to help the children to identify and explore the range of features characteristic of different kinds of persuasive writing, and to contrast them with features of other text types.

The page gives 11 statements describing kinds of persuasive writing and 5 describing the features of chronological recounts. Begin by focusing on the 'The smacking debate'. Ask the children to cut out and select those statements that describe this text. Prompt them to explain their choices, giving examples and reasons.

Repeat this with photocopiable page 5 or 9. A good way of bringing out the comparison is to sort the cut-out statements using a Venn diagram: statements that apply to the first text only, to the second text, and to both.

Children could also use this page independently to analyse examples of persuasive writing and compare them with other text types.

## Features of persuasive writing

Photocopiable page 11 provides a short piece of persuasive writing that illustrates most of the key features of the genre. It is intended for children to use as reference when reading or writing persuasive texts.

## Other activities

Ask the children to find examples of different kinds of persuasive writing. These could be collected in individual or group scrapbooks. They could also look for examples in non-print contexts, such as adverts, speeches, charity appeals, interviews and opinion pieces on television and radio; recording them on video and audio cassettes. These will provide material for the first activity in Section Two.

Display controversial statements about issues of current concern in the class, school, local area or more widely. Ask the children to write short statements expressing agreement, qualified agreement or disagreement.

# How persuasive texts work

Kind of text _____

Point of view _____

_____

| Main arguments | Supporting reasons and evidence |
| --- | --- |
|  |  |
|  |  |
|  |  |

Style and language devices

*writing guides:* **PERSUASIVE WRITING**

# The smacking debate – continued

Read this reply to the letter you looked at earlier. Think about how it is written. Is it similar to the first letter? Finish off the letter, writing two more paragraphs in response to the first letter.

---

Dear Editor

Don't be fooled! The letter you published last week arguing against the tried-and-tested practice of smacking might have persuaded some of your readers. But the writers' case does not hold up to close examination.

    First, they try to show that smacking does not work. Well, this is total nonsense. It certainly does in some cases. If your child was reaching out to touch a hot iron, what would you do? Would you talk with them, and explain the error of their ways? No, of course you wouldn't. You would give their hand a good sharp smack – as quick as you could. And why? Because every sensible parent knows this is the best way of preventing them from hurting themselves. Adults have smacked children for thousands of years because they know it works.

---

# What kind of writing?

Which of these statements describe persuasive writing?

retells what happened

expresses one point of view

starts with an introduction, stating the writer's position

organised chronologically

includes language designed to catch the reader's attention

uses evidence to support an argument

uses words and phrases that make logical connections

mostly written in the present tense

addresses the reader directly

uses words and phrases that make time connections

organised in a series of arguments

uses language to manipulate the reader's ideas and emotions

usually written in the past tense

ends with a conclusion summarising and/or restating the position

about particular people and events

uses typography and design to catch the reader's attention

# Features of persuasive writing

**introduction states the point of view**

**language to gain the reader's attention**

**written in the present tense**

Where shall we go for our school trip?

The answer is staring us in the face. The place to go on this summer's Year 6 school trip is the zoo.

**persuasive devices**

First, it's not too far from the school. Surely no one wants to waste half the day sitting in a smelly, bumpy old coach.

**presents opinion as fact**

Second, there's something interesting for everyone. There are all sorts of animals, fishes, birds and reptiles. The zoo also has beautiful gardens, a woodland walk and an adventure area. We'll have a good time even if it rains because many of the animals are kept indoors.

**detail and explanation support the main point**

**organised as sequence of arguments**

Third, it would be a popular choice. Our survey of Year 6 pupils shows that the zoo is the first choice for 65% and second choice for 20%. Only three children did not want to go to the zoo.

**linking words make logical connections**

Three good reasons for choosing the zoo. Why think about anywhere else?

**use of factual evidence to support the point of view**

**conclusion summarises the point of view**

**rhetorical question**

# SECTION TWO
## DEVELOPING WRITING

*The activities in this section are designed to help children develop their understanding of issues especially relevant to persuasive writing and to use its characteristic features effectively. Each activity gives them an opportunity to focus on and explore a particular aspect of this genre.*

*The activities also give children experience of analysing and writing different kinds of persuasive texts – letters, editorials, advertisements, leaflets and speeches. This will extend their knowledge of the different forms persuasive writing can take and how different forms are suited to different purposes.*

*In Section Three they will draw on these skills and experiences to plan, write and revise sustained pieces of persuasive writing on topics of their own choice.*

## Generating ideas

The first three activities in this section give the children opportunities to explore further the purposes and types of persuasive texts, and to begin to generate topics and ideas in preparation for their own persuasive writing. This involves finding, reading and evaluating persuasive texts; identifying issues that matter to them and on which different views can be taken; and developing views on these issues through discussion, role-play and mini writing activities.

## The language and structure of persuasive texts

The following two photocopiable activities, 'Walk to school' and 'Linking ideas', focus on important stylistic and organisational features of persuasive writing: the use of emotive and manipulative language, the structure of writing that puts a case, and the use of connectives in logical argument. In both cases, the children first examine and work with the text provided and then write something of their own in the same form.

## Fact and opinion

The three photocopiable activities on pages 19–21 focus on a crucial issue in persuasive writing: the distinction between fact and opinion. Children investigate how this distinction can be deliberately blurred and distorted and how facts can be used as the basis for a piece of persuasive writing. They also explore how to counter a particular point of view by the use of opposing facts and opinions.

## Drawing it all together

The final activity, 'Make it better', gives the children an opportunity to draw together and consolidate all that they have learned about persuasive writing. Taking on the role of editor, they evaluate and revise a persuasive text that has many shortcomings. In preparation for the choices they will be making in Section Three, they review the persuasive texts they have read and those they have produced themselves, identifying their different features and the purposes, subjects and contexts for which they are best suited.

*writing guides:* **PERSUASIVE WRITING**

# KINDS OF PERSUASIVE WRITING

## WHAT YOU NEED

A collection of different kinds of persuasive texts, including wordy/text-heavy advertisements, newspaper editorials, letters written for a variety of persuasive purposes, campaign flyers, publicity leaflets; paper and writing materials; board or flip chart.

## WHAT TO DO

If possible, prepare for this activity by asking the children to bring in examples of persuasive texts. Briefly recap on the key issues identified in Section 1.

Ask pairs of children to choose, examine and evaluate a persuasive text from the collection. To support this, you could write up a list of key points, such as purpose, audience, context, structure, language style, and effectiveness. Ask them to prepare to share what they have found out, and to write a label or caption about their chosen text. Organise pairs to present their text to the rest of the class, and prompt other children to ask questions about it. Work together to categorise kinds of persuasive writing related to form (such as letters and adverts) and purpose (such as to complain or protest), and present labelled displays of each type.

### OBJECTIVE
■ To read and evaluate different kinds of persuasive writing and to identify, for each, characteristic features of layout, structure and language.

# TOPICS FOR PERSUASIVE WRITING

## WHAT YOU NEED

Board or flip chart, small whiteboards or scrap paper, writing materials.

## WHAT TO DO

Ask individuals or pairs to brainstorm topics on which views in the class differ. Prompt them to consider a wide range of possibilities, including issues currently under debate in school, locally or more widely; subjects on which decisions have to be made (where to go for a school trip); favourites and preferences (authors, snack foods, pop groups). Briefly share and write up ideas, and choose a topic that seems to be of lively interest to a large number of the class. Give the children a few minutes to develop a point of view about this topic, and then share these in discussion. Encourage them to challenge each other's opinions, for example by asking for clarification or supporting evidence. Develop this through appropriate role-play activities, such as conversations between people with different views or 'balloon debates' (a hot-air balloon contains four people or objects – pop stars or footballers, a mobile phone or handheld computer game and so on; the balloon is losing height and the children debate and vote on what to throw out first, second...).

### OBJECTIVES
■ To identify a range of relevant subjects for persuasive writing.
■ To develop, express and justify opinions through discussion and role-play.

# PERSUASIVE SENTENCES

## WHAT YOU NEED

Small whiteboards or scrap paper, board or flip chart, large sheets and/or strips of paper, writing materials including thick felt-tipped pens.

## WHAT TO DO

Choose a topic on which a range of views are held (if possible return to the one debated in the previous activity), and ask the children to write just one sentence expressing their opinion on it. For example, *Stop animal experiments because they are cruel and useless.* Share these sentences, then write some up for closer examination and discuss their structure and the use of logical connectives (for example, *because*). Consider their clarity and effectiveness, distinguishing between

### OBJECTIVES
■ To express opinions concisely and clearly in writing.
■ To explore sentence- and word-level aspects of persuasive writing, in particular characteristic sentence structures and use of connectives.

*writing guides:* **PERSUASIVE WRITING**

those that simply state an opinion and those that briefly justify it through argument or evidence. How could they be improved or elaborated?

Ask pairs or trios of children to choose a topic of concern or interest to them (for example, one from the list they brainstormed in the previous activity) and to write a banner or poster expressing and justifying their view. Explain that the piece of writing should be short but clear and powerful. Encourage them to explore different formats, for example bullet points, and to experiment with layout. Share and discuss the work and display around the room.

## WALK TO SCHOOL
### WHAT YOU NEED

Photocopiable page 17, paper, scissors, glue, writing materials. If possible, set up the text on computer so that children can reorder by cutting and pasting.

### WHAT TO DO

Briefly review work from Section One on the organisation of texts that argue a point of view. Introduce the children to the jumbled-up letter on the photocopiable page (and/or on computer). Tell them, individually or in pairs, to reorder the statements; find the persuasive devices; and write their own paragraph.

When they have finished, share and compare responses. Identify the introduction and conclusion, and the three arguments, each with its related evidence and or reasons. Discuss the use of fact and opinion and how these are sometimes combined. Consider whether these arguments can be organised in any order.

If possible, make an enlarged version of the text, and ask the children to identify examples of persuasive devices, for example assuming agreement (*Everyone... knows*); exaggeration (*shockingly, devastating, bound to be*); abuse of those who think or behave differently (*selfish and thoughtless*). Discuss the effect of such devices: do they increase the power of the case or backfire?

Share the children's new paragraphs, highlighting use of argument and evidence, where it fits in the letter, and any use of persuasive devices.

## LINKING IDEAS
### WHAT YOU NEED

Photocopiable page 18; a selection of banners that use logical connectives, such as those from 'Persuasive sentences' on page 13; writing materials; paper.

### WHAT TO DO

Read together banners that include sentences with logical connectives, for example *Whaling causes suffering <u>so</u> put an end to it now*. Prompt the children to identify these words and phrases, and discuss their function. Work together to compile a list of other connectives which can be used to link ideas in an argument. Use shared writing techniques to try out some of them in sentences related to topics that the children have been debating in previous activities.

Work through the first sentence on the photocopiable page together, and ask the children to fill in the rest of the gaps. They should then put forward their own view. When they have finished, compare their answers and identify places where only one connective works and others where there are options. Re-read together to check that the text makes sense. Share the children's new paragraphs; identify any connecting words they have used and discuss the clarity, coherence and effectiveness of the argument.

### OBJECTIVES
■ To investigate the structure of texts which present an argument.
■ To identify the use of emotive devices in persuasive writing.

### OBJECTIVES
■ To investigate the use of connecting words and phrases in logical argument.
■ To extend repertoire of such connectives and use them in their own writing.

*writing guides*: **PERSUASIVE WRITING**

# ADVERTISEMENTS
## WHAT YOU NEED
Photocopiable page 19, a collection of advertisements from newspapers and magazines, plain paper, writing materials.

## WHAT TO DO
Ask the children individually to browse the collection of advertisements, choose one and examine how it works, paying special attention to layout and language. Share the findings and prompt the children to identify the 'pitch' of each advertisement and to discuss key issues such as invented words; unconventional spellings; short, verbless sentences; alliteration, rhythm and rhyme; comparatives and superlatives; figurative language; mixing of fact and opinion.

Introduce the photocopiable page and tell the children to underline the words in the advertisements which are used to persuade people to buy the products. They should then write brief notes on a separate piece of paper on how the advertisements work. When the children have completed this, share their ideas and prompt them to consider the issues and techniques noted above.

Then set them to write their own advertisements. Explain that they need to start by identifying their audience (for example, in the case of the CD-ROM encyclopedia, whether children or their parents) and what the main selling point will be. When they have finished, share the advertisements. Discuss layout, use of language, and effectiveness in relation to the chosen audience and selling point.

**OBJECTIVES**
■ To investigate language and layout features of advertisements, focusing on the 'selling point' and the use of persuasive devices.
■ To write their own advertisement.

# STARTING WITH FACTS
## WHAT YOU NEED
Photocopiable page 20, a collection of leaflets and flyers designed for persuasive purposes, plain A4 paper, writing materials.

## WHAT TO DO
Recap on the distinction between fact and opinion, ideally by examining examples in persuasive texts the children have been studying. Distribute the leaflets and flyers, and give the children a few minutes to examine them. Share ideas, focusing on audience and purpose, organisation and presentation. Identify and discuss uses of fact and opinion; how they are related (for example, opinions based on or related to facts); and any attempts to present opinion as fact. Raise the topic of school dinners and packed lunches: ask the children for facts and opinions on this. Again, discuss the distinction between the two and how they can be related.

Introduce the photocopiable page, and ask the children to complete the task; this would work well as a pair activity. During and after this independent work, look for opportunities to discuss issues of fact and opinion, and how information can be organised and presented to create a persuasive effect.

**OBJECTIVE**
■ To develop understanding of the distinction between fact and opinion, the relationship between them, and their roles in persuasive writing.

# I DISAGREE
## WHAT YOU NEED
Photocopiable page 21, writing materials.

## WHAT TO DO
Choose an issue already debated, and briefly present one viewpoint on it. Ask the children to argue against that viewpoint. As the discussion proceeds, draw out the idea that there are two main ways of doing this: through refutation (attacking that

**OBJECTIVE**
■ To explore ways of countering an argument.

point of view, for example by challenging its logic or presenting counter evidence) and by arguing for an opposing view, backing this up with reasons and evidence. Encourage the children to use both approaches.

Introduce the photocopiable activity, telling the children they are going to plan a speech in favour of allowing ball games in the playground. First they need to *counter* the three points detailed in the case for banning ball games, then think of three arguments in favour of allowing them and develop this into a speech. The task should be carried out individually. Afterwards, ask them to make their speeches. Invite others to raise objections and ask questions, drawing on the approaches discussed. Identify and discuss the characteristics of the most persuasive speeches.

## MAKE IT BETTER
### WHAT YOU NEED
Photocopiable page 22, board or flip chart, writing materials.

### WHAT TO DO
Briefly review texts from Section One, particularly the poster on page 11, and together identify those which provide good examples of the genre. Compile and record a list of criteria for effective persuasive writing, including clarity of structure and argument, use of relevant evidence, powerful but non-manipulative language.

Introduce the photocopiable page, explaining that this attempt at a persuasive text has many shortcomings. Read the first few paragraphs and discuss some of the problems. Then ask the children to complete both parts of the task individually or in pairs. Emphasise that in writing their own paragraphs they should make just one point in favour of or against school uniforms as clearly and powerfully as they can.

When they have finished, share the notes to the author. If possible, make an enlarged text version of the piece, and highlight and annotate this to indicate the problems. Then ask some children to read their paragraphs about school uniforms. Evaluate and discuss these, referring to the list of criteria compiled earlier.

## BRINGING IT ALL TOGETHER
### WHAT YOU NEED
Board or flip chart.

### WHAT TO DO
Drawing on earlier work, compile a list of different kinds of persuasive writing: letters, newspaper comment, speeches in debates, advertisements, campaign leaflets. Prompt the children to discuss the strengths and weaknesses of each type, focusing on their appropriateness for particular purposes and audience. What is each kind of text especially good for?

Return to an issue previously discussed in this section or introduce a new one (for example, encouraging children to watch less television), and ask the class to imagine that they are planning a campaign. Identify different audiences to which this campaign might be addressed (children, parents, the wider community), different ways of achieving its aims (for example, through detailed argument or images and short statements with lots of impact), and different formats. As the discussion proceeds, record ideas as a concept map and encourage the children to focus on the issue of appropriateness: the match between purpose, audience and format.

Explain that they will now be going on to plan, develop and write a campaign on an issue of their own choice (see Section Three).

### OBJECTIVES
■ To evaluate the effectiveness of a persuasive text.
■ To construct an argument to persuade others to a point of view.

### OBJECTIVES
■ To explore the appropriateness of different kinds of persuasive writing in relation to audience and purpose.
■ To prepare for the decisions they need to make when planning and writing persuasive texts independently.

# Walk to school

Someone has started drafting a letter to the local newspaper on the computer but the ideas are still jumbled up.

**1.** Cut out the pieces and arrange them in the best order.
**2.** When you have done this, underline the words and phrases the writer uses to persuade people of her point of view.
**3.** Then write another paragraph for the letter.

Everyone with children at Pitchford knows just how congested and dangerous the roads around the school become at the beginning and end of the school day.

I do hope that all parents will cooperate in this new scheme – for the benefit of their children's health, of road safety, and of the environment. Surely it's not too much to ask.

Some drivers are so selfish and thoughtless that they even park on the pavements, with the result that pedestrians are forced to walk in the road.

Recent research shows that many children take shockingly little exercise.

Particles in vehicle emissions can have a devastating effect on health, especially for people already suffering from heart or lung problems.

Sooner or later there is bound to be a serious accident, maybe even a fatality.

I am writing to express my support for the 'Walk to school' campaign being organised by parents and staff at Pitchford Street School.

Leaving your car at home will help reduce this major cause of air pollution.

Walking to school will help to avoid health problems in adult life.

# Linking ideas

Below is part of a newspaper editorial about experiments using animals. Fill the gaps with these connecting words or phrases to link the ideas. You will need to use some of them more than once.

> *also*　*although*　*instead*　*but*　*because*　*for example*
>
> *and*　*however*　*unless*　*as a result of*　*therefore*　*if*

Supporters of animal experiments claim that advances in science and medicine will stop _____ such experiments continue. They say that researchers minimise suffering _____ insist that it is a price we have to pay. They point out that life-saving drugs are available only _____ they were tested on animals. They argue that our knowledge of the human body has increased _____ investigations into the bodies of other vertebrates. They conclude that progress depends on animal research, and that _____ it must continue.

_____, this case gets weaker by the day. The argument may be strong when applied to medicines, _____ most experiments on animals concern cosmetics, food additives and weapons. Surely the price is not worth paying _____ the result is better bullets or more colourful fruit juices.

It is increasingly clear that _____ experiments on animals can provide valuable information about humans, they can _____ be misleading. _____, penicillin saves human lives _____ kills guinea pigs; wine and beer make humans drunk _____ have no effect on rats _____ rats break down alcohol more quickly.

Fortunately, there is a solution to the dilemma: use computers _____ of animals.

Now write a paragraph putting forward your own view about experiments on animals.

*writing guides:* PERSUASIVE WRITING

# Advertisements

Underline the words in these advertisements used to persuade people to buy the products. Write a short note explaining how each advertisement works.

**UNMISSABLE BARGAIN!!!**

CARRON X02

THE FAST AND FABULOUS **CARRON X02** – THE ULTIMATE GAMES MACHINE EASY TO SET UP AND USE. COMES COMPLETE WITH 10 OF YOUR ALL-TIME FAVOURITE GAMES, INCLUDING THE MIND-BENDING **ELEVATOR** AND THE THRILLING **RACE TIME 2**. HOURS OF FUN GUARANTEED.

Only £70

**BIGGEST SAVINGS EVER!**

**TOTTERING TOWERS**

How high? What shape?
A game that's guaranteed to give all the family hours of fascinating fun.

**30 PIECES** beautifully crafted in wood.

**SNACKEROOS**

The breakthrough in taste sensation.
Full of flavour. Full of goodness.
In four delicious flavours.
Made from only the finest natural ingredients.

Write advertisements for a children's encyclopedia on CD-ROM and a mini-scooter. Think about how to use words to get people interested and make them want to buy.

# Starting with facts

A local education authority is planning a leaflet to persuade parents to use their school meals service. They have started out by listing facts about the service they provide and school meals in general.

- at least two 'main meal' choices every day

- daily 'main meals' nutritionally balanced

- varied menus

- menus include less familiar foods for children to try

- a hot meal offered every day

- a vegetarian option offered every day

- most dishes cooked using fresh ingredients

- no packaging, and so is the environmental choice

- no need to spend time shopping for and preparing packed lunches if your child has school meals

- a school meal often costs less than a packed lunch and offers good value for money

Use these facts as the basis for drafting a leaflet aimed at persuading parents to choose school meals instead of packed lunches. You will need to add new ideas and decide how best to organise the information on the leaflet.

Take an A4 sheet of paper and fold it into three – like this:

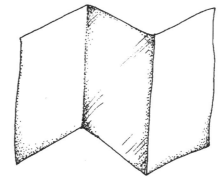

# I disagree

Class HF were having a debate about ball games in the school playground. Here are the three main points for the side arguing **against** ball games.

- First, ball games take up too much space. This is unfair to other children.
- Second, ball games are dangerous. Other children often get knocked over or hit by the ball.
- Third, ball games cause arguments and can lead to fighting.

Use these bubbles to plan a speech in favour of ball games.

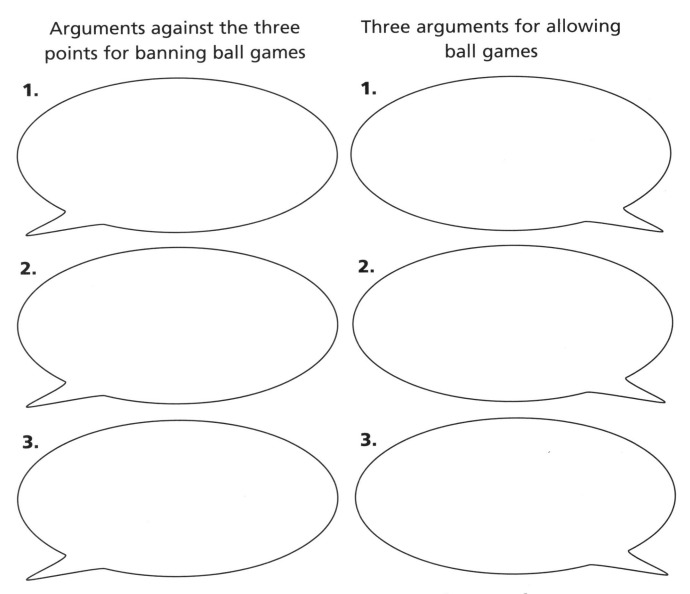

Arguments against the three points for banning ball games

Three arguments for allowing ball games

1.

1.

2.

2.

3.

3.

Use your notes to help you write the speech.

# Make it better

Imagine that you are the editor of a class newspaper. Someone gives you this first draft of an editorial about school uniforms.

*link?*

I don't like school uniforms. They make everyone look the same. Nobody likes wearing them. ———

*How does the writer know this?*

The same colour doesn't suit everybody. It's really horrible having to wear the same old clothes every day. Ties are old-fashioned and lots of children can't do them up properly.

When we take off our sweatshirts for PE, they get mixed up. They say that uniforms look smart, but they get scruffy if you wear them all the time.

My sister says she doesn't like wearing red.

Sometimes children grab each other's ties and pull them hard.

Some people say that school uniforms make you feel proud, and when we go on a visit everyone knows that we are from Pitchford Street School, but I don't agree.

So school uniforms are a bad idea and we should be able to wear what we like, but if we have to wear a uniform it should be blue not red.

Write a note to the author explaining the problems with this piece of writing and how to improve it. You can write on and around the text itself as well – some examples have been done for you. Think about:
- how the piece of writing is organised
- how ideas are connected
- the use of argument and evidence to support this point of view.

Now write a paragraph putting one argument for or against school uniforms to show the writer how it should be done!

*writing guides:* **PERSUASIVE WRITING**

*The photocopiable pages in this section are designed to support children as they plan, draft and present their own pieces of persuasive writing. They guide children through different stages in the writing process and prompt them to consider issues of form and content that are especially relevant to this kind of writing. The first two double-page spreads offer different approaches to generating and developing ideas that can then be followed up by pages 28 and 29.*

## Animal experiments

The support offered on photocopiable pages 24–5 is subject-specific, and based on the controversial issue of experiments on animals. The focus is on helping the children generate and begin organising ideas in preparation for more detailed planning of the piece. The first page of the spread offers a range of facts and opinions related to this issue. The second page provides a framework to help the children develop arguments and evidence for their own position on the issue, and to counter opposing arguments. This spread will be of particular use to children who need help in getting started on this writing activity. It also provides material that will help children to develop an argument more fully.

## Make your point

The activity on photocopiable pages 26–7 is relevant to any issue and would be more suitable for those children who do not need as much help in getting started. A framework of questions highlights decisions that need to be made in developing a piece of persuasive writing, including choice of topic; stating and developing a point of view; considering opposing views; gathering evidence; considering persuasive techniques and emphases. The children are asked to develop their point of view using a web diagram.

## Planning and presenting persuasive texts

Photocopiable page 28 is a planner for extended persuasive writing. It helps the children organise more systematically the ideas they generated using the earlier photocopiable activities. It is most suitable for forms such as letters, essays, speeches and editorials. The structure prompts the children not just to state arguments but to elaborate them through explanation and/or evidence.

Photocopiable page 29 asks the children to consider and choose between different ways in which persuasive writing can be presented. In doing so it relates back to the range examined in activities in Sections One and Two. Some of these (letter, editorial) involve extended, organised prose. Others (advertisement, leaflet, poster) give scope for the use of images, design and typography as persuasive devices. Encourage the children to consider what would be most appropriate for their purpose and their audience. For example, if they want to make a long, detailed argument, then a letter or editorial might be suitable. If they want to communicate just a few key ideas powerfully, and perhaps even to shock, then a leaflet or poster might be more suitable.

Over a more extended period, children could use both of these photocopiable pages to help them plan a 'campaign' to promote their point of view, and write a range of materials in different forms.

# Animal experiments

Use these facts and opinions to help you work out your own ideas about experiments on animals.

## Facts

● Experiments on animals have led directly to the development of new treatments for diseases and new surgical procedures.

● More than 50% of animal experiments are carried out on mice and rats. These animals are classified as vermin, and often routinely killed.

● Experiments on animals are used to test a variety of products including food colourings, cleaning products, shampoos, medicines and weapons.

● The results of animal experiments can be misleading. For example, the drug thalidomide caused deformities in humans but not in the rats on which it was tested.

● Most animals used in experiments are bred specifically for this purpose, and never know life outside a laboratory.

● The law requires many products to be tested to ensure their safety before they can be put on sale.

● There are laws regulating experiments on animals. Scientists have to explore alternative methods, use the minimum number of animals, and ensure that they suffer minimum distress.

● The number of experiments using animals is falling as alternative methods, eg computer-modelling, are discovered.

## Opinions

It is never right to cause deliberate suffering to an animal – no matter what the reason.

Experiments on animals are justified only when they concern the treatment of diseases.

Tests should be carried out on animals only when all alternatives have been tried.

It's all right to use rats and mice, but not cats, dogs or monkeys.

If it's all right to kill animals for food, then why not for scientific experiments?

The needs of human beings come before those of the lower animals.

My view on animal experiments.

_____

_____

| Arguments for this view | Facts to support these arguments |
|---|---|
| 1. | |
| 2. | |
| 3. | |

| Opposing points of view | Arguments and evidence to counter these views |
|---|---|
| 1. | |
| 2. | |
| 3. | |

# Make your point

**1.** What issues do you have strong opinions about? Write a list.

_____     _____

_____     _____

_____     _____

Choose one! _____

**2.** What is your point of view on this issue? Write your point of view in the centre of this web diagram and supporting arguments and evidence in the circles radiating outwards.

*writing guides:* PERSUASIVE WRITING

**3.** What other points of view do people have on this issue?

| Some people think | I'd say to them |
|---|---|

**4.** What do you need to find out more about? How could you find out?

_____

_____

_____

_____

**5.** How will you persuade people to take your side on this issue? What are the key points? What strategies could you use?

_____

_____

_____

_____

# Planner for persuasive writing

Introduction/statement of your point of view

_____

_____

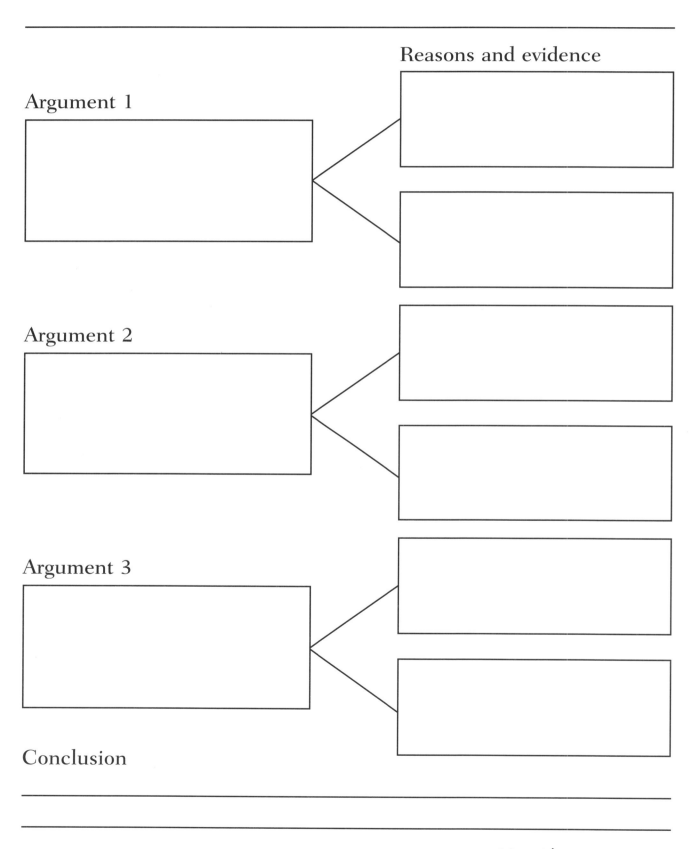

Argument 1

Reasons and evidence

Argument 2

Argument 3

Conclusion

_____

_____

*writing guides:* **PERSUASIVE WRITING**

# Formats and presentation

What form will your writing take? Think about what would be most suitable for your audience and your purpose.

**a letter?**
to whom?
What do they think about the issue?
How will you persuade them
to your point of view?

**a poster?**
How will you grab people's attention?
What images will you use?
Will you use any key words or phrases?

**a newspaper editorial?**
What will the headline be?
How will you organise your ideas?
Will you include factual evidence?

**a leaflet?**
How many sides will it have?
What will people read first?
What will they read next?
Will you use persuasive devices?

**an advertisement for TV or radio?**
Will it be a dialogue between characters?
Or will you use a voiceover?
What will the pictures show?

# SECTION FOUR
## REVIEW

*In this section the writing process comes full circle as children apply what they learned in Section One about the qualities of effective persuasive texts to reviewing and revising their own writing. The focus for review relates closely to the issues that they explored in Section Two: structure and coherence, layout and presentation, countering other views, effective use of argument and evidence, forceful writing making use of persuasive devices. The review also gives children an opportunity to consider how effectively they have carried out the plans and fulfilled the purposes they set out in Section Three.*

## Using the photocopiable pages

Photocopiable pages 31 and 32 pose three big questions about persuasive writing for the children to consider:
● Is my argument clear?
● Is the text well organised?
● Are my arguments forceful?
Each of these questions is teased out by means of a series of more sharply focused questions that prompt the children to review aspects of their writing closely and critically. The third of these relates to forcefulness, the key issue in persuasive writing, and develops it at more length. Beneath each question there is space for the children to make short notes. Encourage them to provide examples from their own writing. Some of the questions will be more or less relevant depending on the form in which the children have written, for example questions about organisation in paragraphs will be more relevant to a piece of extended prose than to a poster. These review questions are followed by one that prompts the children to consider the next step: improving what they have written. Again, there is space for notes.

## Supporting the children's work

You could introduce and support independent use of these photocopiable pages by working through one of the questions with the children. A good way of going about this is to choose a piece of writing with illuminating strengths and weaknesses as an example. First, help the children to examine and make judgements about it in relation to the points raised in the questions. In particular, prompt them to go beyond yes/no responses to analyse the nature and causes of any weaknesses. Secondly, in the light of these judgements, prompt them to identify ways of improving the writing, checking that they really do address the problems identified. Thirdly, use shared-writing techniques to revise the text and implement some of these improvements.

## Assessing the children's persuasive writing

Use the questions on the photocopiable pages when assessing children's progress and achievement in persuasive writing, and to set targets for further development. Look in particular for growing ability:
● to put forward an argument clearly and coherently, and to elaborate and support it with logical reasoning and evidence
● to write eloquently and forcefully – this is indicated by powerful words and by the use of sentence structures that keep the writing lively, for example short sentences for effect, balanced or similar structures, rhythm.

# Reviewing your persuasive writing (1)

## Is my argument clear?

- Are the main points set out clearly?

- Are ideas clearly and logically linked? Have I used connecting words or phrases (such as **however, but**)?

- How can I improve the clarity of my argument?

## Is the text well organised?

- Is there an introduction? Is it effective?

- Is there a conclusion? Is it effective?

- Are ideas organised in paragraphs?

- Does each paragraph have a clear focus?

- How can I improve the organisation of the text?

# Reviewing your persuasive writing (2)

## Are my arguments forceful?

● Have I supported my points with reasons and explanations?

● Have I supported my points with evidence? Is the evidence relevant?

● Have I taken opposing points of view into account? Have I argued against them?

● Have I used powerful words?

● Have I thought about my audience? (What they know, what their opinion is and how best to persuade them.)

● How can I make my argument more forceful?